April 2011

Hermana Dolores

Thank you for your great encouragement and support during the writing process, and always. I hope you enjoy these poems.

~Ray

We Had More to Say
Poems from the Pilgrimage Road

Praise for
We Had More to Say

"Ortiz's poems expand the idea of pilgrimage to include those experiences which touch some profound dimension within, when connections are made with what might be called "soul" or "spirit," when the tourist becomes the seeker, and sight-seeing magically turns into soul-making. The sacred journey takes us to those liminal places where one dimension touches another. Among many skills and themes, this poet favors transformation: extending the commonplace like a quilt, a grave stone, his grandfather's shovel into the margins between memory and the sacred. There are many love poems in which the present moment shifts into something grand, wide or deep. The poems in We Had More to Say are also a vivid testimony to how grief or loss can be turned into a blessing. They shift and blend, and meld into another dimension. People move in and out of reality."

—David M. Johnson, Professor Emeritus,
English and creative writing, University of New Mexico.
Author of *Rebirth of Wonder: Poems of the Common Life*

"There is an uncommon humanity so evident in the poetry of Ray Ortiz that, reading it, I feel restored to my own family, my ancestors, and my own homeland. For Ortiz is a poet who upholds the ancient goals of civilization —to preserve the tribe, to praise its flourishing, to lament its sorrows. There is great bearing in his words, a dignity in his descriptions of life felt simply and deeply that, once recognized, travels to his reader and bears him up like a child riding on the shoulders of a great elder. We Had More to Say is a book of utterly civilized vision and humane plenty that, having just read it, is a blessing more than enough."

—Garrett Hongo, author of *Volcano: A Memoir of Hawai`i*

We Had More to Say
Poems from the Pilgrimage Road

Raymond Zachary Ortiz

SANTA FE

© 2011 by Raymond Zachary Ortiz.
All Rights Reserved.

No part of this book may be reproduced in any form or by any electronic or mechanical means including information storage and retrieval systems without permission in writing from the publisher, except by a reviewer who may quote brief passages in a review.

Sunstone books may be purchased for educational, business, or sales promotional use. For information please write: Special Markets Department, Sunstone Press, P.O. Box 2321, Santa Fe, New Mexico 87504-2321.

Book design by Vicki Ahl
Body typeface > Humanst521 BT
Printed on acid free paper

Library of Congress Cataloging-in-Publication Data

Ortiz, Raymond Zachary, 1953-
  We had more to say : poems from the pilgrimage road / by Raymond Zachary Ortiz.
      p. cm.
  ISBN 978-0-86534-763-2 (pbk. : alk. paper)
  I. Title.
  PS3615.R83W4 2011
  811'.6--dc22
                                                    2011003715

WWW.SUNSTONEPRESS.COM
SUNSTONE PRESS / POST OFFICE BOX 2321 / SANTA FE, NM 87504-2321 /USA
(505) 988-4418 / ORDERS ONLY (800) 243-5644 / FAX (505) 988-1025

Dedication

To my grandfathers Ramón and Zacarías for giving me your love of life and poetry;

to my grandmothers Stella and Dorothy for your inspiration and mystery; and

to my parents Thomas and Ida for your depth of feeling and quiet strength.

Between my finger and my thumb
The squat pen rests; snug as a gun.

Under my window, a clean rasping sound
When the spade sinks into gravelly ground:
My father, digging. I look down....

By God, the old man could handle a spade.
Just like his old man.....

But I've no spade to follow men like them.

Between my finger and my thumb
The squat pen rests.
I'll dig with it.

—Excerpts from the poem "Digging" in
Death of a Naturalist by Seamus Heaney

CONTENTS

FOREWORD—11
ACKNOWLEDGMENTS—15

AWAKENING—17

Friends—19
How Many Miracles?—21
Death and Life—22
The First Time—23
Journey Around the World—24
Whispers Through the Night—25
Did I Know You?—26
Back to Life—27
Walking Arm-In-Arm Into the Storm—28
Three Faces of the Night—29
What Part of Light?—30

PILGRIMAGE LANDSCAPES—31

Two Rivers—33
Landscapes—34
Conversation With My Soul—35
Sometimes We Wander Away—37
Plains of Castilla—38
Reflections—39
Humble Water—40
Into the Labyrinth—41
The Laying of Hands—43
Rising Out of the Canyon—44
Slowly Parting—46
How Do I Say Good Bye?—47
Irises—49
Living in Two Worlds—50
In a Spring in a Storm—51
I Find Myself Looking for You—53
Flight 1010—54
First Train to Chicago—55
Vine by the Seashore—57
Fishing for Truth—59

Touching Joy—61
Ode to Apricots—62
Lighthouse of God—64
View from Joy–66

LOOKING HOME—67

Floating—69
Letter to My Son—72
Finding My Father—73
Helping Ida—75
Ode to My Quilt—77
Tending the Dead—80
You Are the Gift—82
That Last Evening—83
To My Child Never Born—84
Gratitude—86
You Are Inside Me —87
Gazing Toward the Horizon of Hope—88
My Son Is Coming Home—89
Ode to My Shovel—90

NEW PASSAGES—93

We Saw the Moon Rise—95
Passages—97
Gather All of Yourself—98
Thanksgiving—99
I Want to Dance—100
What Is This Longing?—101
Quiet Courage—102
How Long?—103
I Will Be With You—105
Let Your Sweetness In—106
Fifty—107
Blessings—109
Stories of Our Lives—110
I Thought I Knew Love—112
Coming Home—113
We Had More to Say—115

ABOUT THE AUTHOR—117

We Had More to Say

Poems from the Pilgrimage Road

FOREWORD

Three poems in Ray Ortiz's excellent collection, *We Had More to Say*, set out the motifs that will be woven in and out of other pieces throughout the entire book. "How Many Miracles" explores the importance of ancestry, the workings of chance or fate, the elements of ocean, air, light, and darkness, and the miraculous emerging of the microscopic with the universe. "I Will Be With You" points to a number of deaths that must be faced, honored, and resolved, until finally in the "heaven of memories," father and mother "gaze upon you / from the eyes of your children." Then in "Irises" the color purple, once associated with the passion and sensuality of an O'Keefe painting, is transformed into the "hard purple draped over caskets, / over love buried in the ground."

In "Journey Around the World" birth itself is a "passage out of the tunnel," as is the last transition in death, and, of course, all the experiences in between: the movement from one life stage to another, as well as the detours and dead-ends. The use of the ghazal form provides a satisfying completeness in each stanza, while adding a layered effect by the end of the poem. A recognizable body of images attends the journey motif in this and other poems: rivers separating and converging, mountains and canyons, arrivals and departures, longing and discovery.

A certain kind of travel becomes the sandpaper that rubs away the commonplace and the habitual. The journey provides the freedom to think and feel in new and innovative ways. When we leave the safeguards of habit and the ordinary, we begin to pay attention, to see with both eyes and heart. In "Passages" the poet takes stalk of his journeys and reminds the reader that the novelties of travel can arouse the search for "more intimate places / where I feel grace pulsing in my blood, / where I see the faces of God everywhere."

Ortiz's poems reveal how the ordinary pathways of life are transformed into the wonder and awe of the sacred pilgrimage. A narrow definition of "pilgrimage" suggests a journey made by a pilgrim to an established religious shrine, such as Lourdes in France or Our Lady of Guadalupe north of Mexico City. But Ortiz's poems expand the idea of pilgrimage to include those experiences which touch some profound dimension within, when connections are made with what might be called "soul" or "spirit," when the tourist becomes the seeker, and sight-seeing magically turns into soul-making. The sacred journey takes us to those liminal places where one dimension touches another. As a place of many edges, New Mexico has such potential for the spiritual journey, where one terrain blends into another, where desert meets mountain, and canyons give birth to rivers and lakes.

Ortiz understands how the quest is impeded by the heavy weight of experience that we carry around inside, how in "Friends" we carry sacks and sacks of metaphorical rocks that must be emptied before we are light enough to follow our dreams. It is possible to lose one's way, as in "Sometimes We Wander Away" when "for years and years, we take our direction / from semblances, misconceptions, fantasies, mirages," but then after the fog and dark valleys, we find a new direction "inspired by wind traces, / drawn by the scent of water and mountain light...."

Pilgrimages are difficult, filled with suffering and surprises, those unexpected corners where the pilgrim confronts the inner reality of loneliness and doubt. As the poet admits in "Fifty," "I am in darkness reaching for light." And in "How Long?" the question: "When does / the darkness of coal awaken to the clarity of a diamond?" With "To My Child Never Born," the residue of pain attends each line, but what is admirable is that the poet moves through grief to a kind of miraculous resolution at the end of the poem: "You are inside me, seeing with my eyes, / vibrant with each beat of my heart."

The difficulties of passage are redeemed by moments of discovery, where "In a Spring in a Storm," a remote hot spring becomes a womb world and rebirth:

> As my grateful body uncurls out of the water,
> I am born again into a different kind of religion,
> one of becoming intimate with the earth,
> of touching her and being touched...

When in "Vine by the Seashore" a deep sense of sadness leads to a recognition:

> There is happiness and there is loss,
> intertwined like branches of a great vine
> reaching up, supported only by hope
> and by gnarled roots deeply set
> in the earth of our beings....

Among many skills and themes, this poet favors transformation: extending the commonplace like a quilt, a grave stone, his grandfather's shovel into the margins between memory and the sacred. There are many love poems in which the present moment shifts into something grand, wide or deep. The poems in *We Had More to Say* are also a vivid testimony to how grief or loss can be turned into a blessing, when the "you" in a poem seems to shift from lover into a deity, when in "Finding My Father" his father, permanently scarred by war, is finally "taken by the kind reaper of death / who visited after you had already died a thousand deaths." The poems shift and blend, and meld into another dimension. People move in and out of reality, as the uncle in "Floating" who floats in and out of dreams transformed into a vision:

> I see you rising above the crowd, focused,
> intense, seeing what others could not see;
> releasing a busy life in the city,
> guiding yourself to a serene monastery,
> isolated in a mountain valley,
> vowing to be closer to God, who is inside.

—David M. Johnson, Professor Emeritus,
English and creative writing at
University of New Mexico

ACKNOWLEDGMENTS

To David Johnson and Garrett Hongo for showing me the path of a writer and encouraging me along the way.

Grateful acknowledgment is made to the editors of following publications in which these poems appeared, although in some cases in a different form:

Off the Record, an anthology of poetry by lawyers (Morgantown, West Virginia: The Legal Studies Forum, College of Law, West Virginia University, 2004): "Friends," "Death and Life," "We Had More to Say," "View from Joy" and "How Do I Say Good Bye?"

Man Alive! A Journal of Men's Wellness (Albuquerque, New Mexico: Men's Network Press): "Ode to My Shovel," "Conversation with My Soul," "Death and Life," "Back to Life," "Letter to My Son," "Finding My Father," "Gather All of Yourself," "I Will Be With You," "I Thought I Knew Love" and "Fifty."

Scenes from the Live Poets' Society (Santa Fe: Live Poets' Society, 2003 and 2007) : "Two Rivers," "Death and Life," "Letter to My Son," "Gratitude," "Ode to My Shovel," "Gather All of Yourself," "I Thought I Knew Love," "Gifts," "Blessings," "Ode to My Quilt," "You Are Inside Me," "My Son Is Coming Home" and "Journey Around the World."

Sufi Journal (London: Khaniqahi Nimatullahi publications, Winter, 2001): "Did I Know You?"

Finally, excerpts from the Seamus Heaney poem "Digging" set out at page 3 herein are taken from *Death of a Naturalist* (London: Faber and Faber Ltd., 1966), pp. 13–14 and *Selected Poems, 1966–1987* (New York: Farrar, Straus and Giroux, 1990), pp. 3–4.

AWAKENING

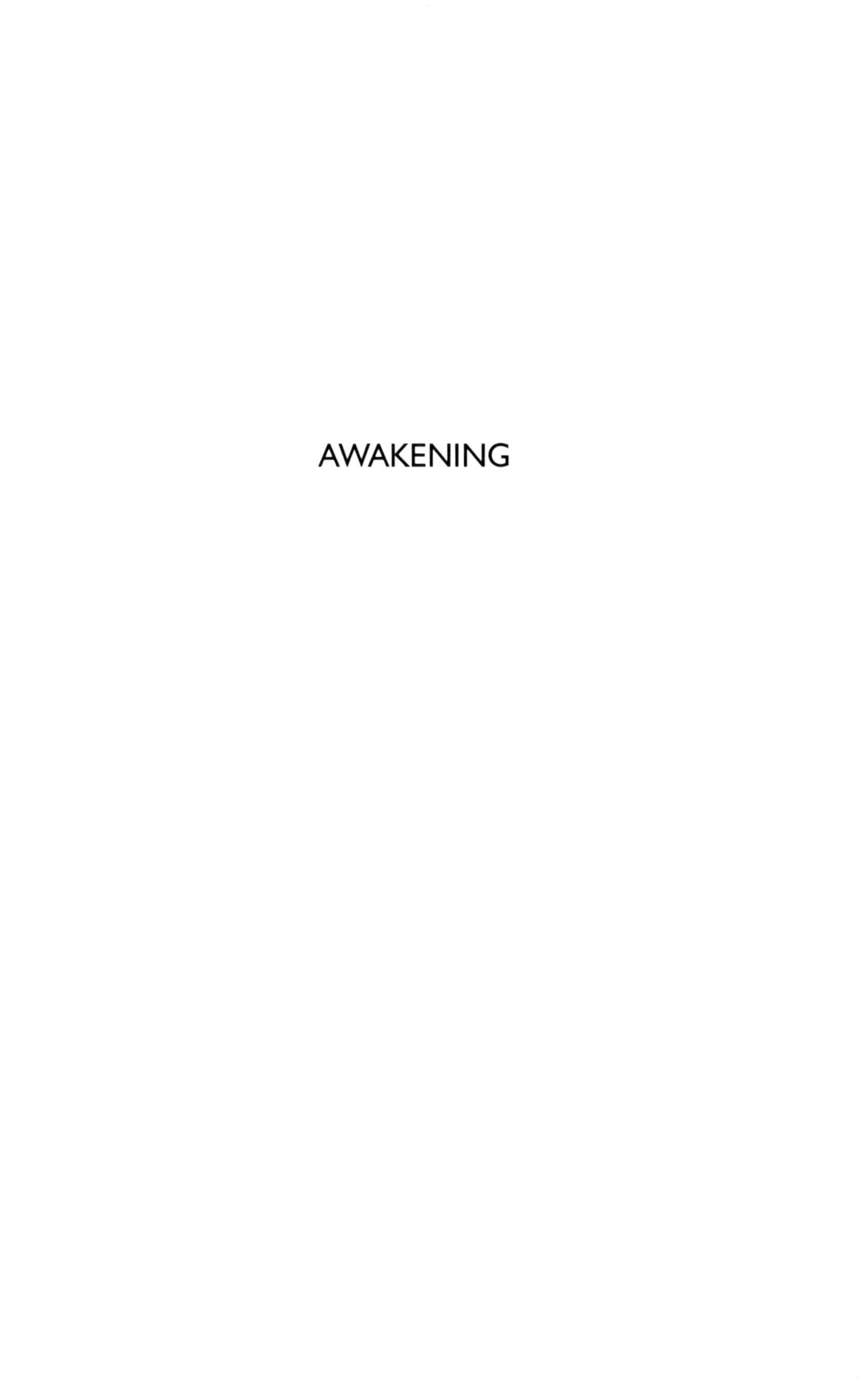

Friends

We gather our problems
up into a large bundle
and throw the load
over our reluctant shoulders
for all the world to see.
Our minds go out
over the rocky fields
carefully turning over
every cumbersome stone,
gathering the most dense,
jagged and irregular pieces
that our bodies,
in their wisdom,
are hesitant to bear.

The blind miser in the field,
accustomed to his hoarding ways,
cannot distinguish gold from lead
and furiously gathers gray weight
until he wears his tangled back
as his proud badge of honor,
thinking he is carrying treasures
instead of dark, confusing heaps
cast off by wise travelers ahead.

We bring sacks and sacks
into our peaceful houses
until there is no room to sleep,
no place to relax with our lovers;
but we are aimlessly content
because the edges of the world
would curl up into earthquakes
if not for the bundles
holding everything in place.

Whisper me your secrets
and I will whisper you mine,
then we will weave them into webs
worthy of gathering dreams
and winds from a mysterious sea.

Instead of a gray world in our sacks
we will carry clouds and dreams
and a few polished stones
as reminders of our aspirations.

We will ourselves be carried
by gentle waves of light
touching the wispy web sails
of our nimble little boat,
guided by a vague coastline
and a phantom compass
with markings we cannot yet name.

How Many Miracles?

How many miracles
did it take to create you?
The chance of love
one stormy night
when your father and mother
should have tended their flock.
Their chance meeting
in a crowded village;
the first enchanted encounter
of their parents in the forest,
and of their parents at sea;
of all your relations.

The chance union
of two wandering cells
in the murky ocean depths.
The chance union
of air into water,
of light into air,
of darkness into light,
of dust into a planet;
the explosion of stars
into the universe
that is inside you.
How many miracles?

Death and Life

They say that when death comes,
those you have loved
gently hold your hand as
life passes before your eyes.

I say that when you came to me,
all of those I have loved
came together in your eyes
as life laid itself out before me.

The First Time

I was a quiet, innocent poet,
minding my business with the shadows,
when you walked out in front of me,
guided by the grace of an angel.

You brought light into the dark forest,
spread fresh colors of the rainbow
over grateful flowers in the meadow.
With a gentle gasp, my breath stood still,
suspended in the eternity of your beauty.

The color of your eyes took me back
to the first dawn seen by a man and a woman
as they looked into each other's souls
and saw reflections of God in the new light.

Journey Around the World

The lull between waves suggests form to each, rhythm.
As they gather their belongings before moving,
each reflects on its being, motion asking for pause.

A conversation: the leader and his advisors,
the priest and his accuser, wind and the ocean.
In each exchange, a halting, glimpse, silence, a pause.

Lovers stop on a bridge, take in starlight swirling
on the river, taste promise on each other's lips,
yearn in between kisses, in the intimate pause.

Seconds pass time between them. In their ambitions
are years, histories waiting, junctures in stories:
a glance, a shot, a passing between centuries, pause.

Between embrace and caress, after conception,
just before passage out of the tunnel at birth,
at the very last breath before death, a quiet pause.

On each journey around the world, the moon searches
for light, gathers herself before peeking over
horizons: before rising, allows time to pause.

Whispers Through the Night

Out from the shore of silence the pilgrim who has walked
a thousand miles sees ocean light on the waves' facets, yearns
for the jewel island of the sea. What is this longing?

In lucid conversations all through the day and night,
on a journey to the places where youth once lived,
where ancestors rest in the ground, what is this longing?

A sailor uses the ocean, a poet an ocean of words
to search in dreams for places where calm light might be,
to search for truth, the one love. What is this longing?

In the lonely spaces between sighs, poems and letters,
the eternity between encounters, the repose between
reflections past and what could be, what is this longing?

On the precipice a cry goes up the dark canyon,
the echo is the hopeful messenger and the message
with a response, a question. What is this longing?

What is this happiness that swirls with the breeze at dawn,
that becomes whispers and deep sighs all through the night,
yearning for a messenger; what is this longing?

Did I Know You?

Your familiar eyes,
kindred light
and intimate soul
take me back
inside time.

Did I meet you
one day as we walked
to pray at the church
made of sand, salt,
and the infinite sound of waves?

Were you with me
when I was young,
a fisherman, a miner, a poet:
searching for truth
in water, in the ground, in dreams?

Did I know you?
Were you my friend,
my companion, my soul mate
from another place,
from another time?

Back to Life

A woman falls by the road
in a lonely accident
at night, in winter.
Her heart is still,
her breath frozen
as the snow on which she lays.
An angel comes to her,
dressed as a passerby,
borrows a breath from God
and blows it lovingly
onto the embers of her life.
Her grateful eyes open
to the still darkness
which eventually gives way
to the gentle light of dawn.

A man walks aimlessly in a forest.
Inside, he is not far from dead.
He heads towards an array of cliffs,
invisible to him in his obsessions.
He cannot smell the arrival of the sea,
is unable to feel the ebb of his heart,
is deaf to the pleas of his soul.
He stops, lays down to rest,
his own tiredness saving him
by bringing him his dreams.
There he converses with God,
dressed as a generous stranger,
who asks discerning questions
that are answered by light
as it illuminates the way.

Walking Arm-in-Arm Into the Storm

After the fire burned for a while in the cave
Plato made sense of all the flickering shadows.
A few more sticks on the fire, awe, enlightening.

Brick by brick they very carefully built a certain
kind of happiness in their separate lives. In act two, the
curtain rose with Zeus raining down bolts of lightning.

The clouds blew in, a dark rain chased us from fields
we had just plowed. The storm gave way to the sun.
Earth's colors, our free hearts, brightened: a lightening.

After this longing deepens, your call late at night,
your long letter from the other side of the world:
your voice, your words, your clear unbound spirit, lightning.

On moving day we pack up pictures, books, plaques, life.
Memories ebb and flow, waves on a rainy beach,
until the sun brings a rainbow, a lightening.

We walked arm-in-arm into the storm, collars
turned against the wind, until we found a tiny
hollow and huddled against fear: all around us lightning.

Three Faces of the Night

1.
Last night, in my dreams,
I told you my life's story.
As you listened with your heart
a path opened up, wide enough for two.

2.
Last night, I saw you again.
You have been with me always,
in my first memories,
as I took my first steps,

As I walked through forests of doubt
thirsty for love that flowed in the ground,
as I walked with death and buried my father,
as I awakened to the beauty of the world.

3.
Last night, I came to you
as fast as truth could carry me
across ambitious mountains,
wandering rivers and lonely plains.

The kind glow of your heart
graced the snowy horizon,
a distant, enchanting city
standing up to darkness.

I came to you as you slept,
embracing your warmth.
Could you feel me close to you?
I came as near as a hundred miles.

What Part of Light?

What part of light
did I see in the radiant glow
of the universe rising inside you?

Was it the color of kindness,
embracing beggars in the streets,
holding those with life's afflictions?

Was it the color of truth,
looking through opaque mountains,
feeling rivers flowing underground?

Was it the color of sorrow,
kneeling under the weight of tears,
praying humbly at the altar of loss?

Was it the color of joy,
beckoning to immigrants from the shore,
glimmering from the height of stars?

Perhaps the color of heaven,
reflecting shades of yearning
slowly welling up inside me.

Each ray was a path of light
followed by pilgrims of the heart,
until we reached soul depth.

The colors joined there, not at light speed,
but in a slow hue of abiding movement,
a crack forming on granite
signaling momentous change.

PILGRIMAGE LANDSCAPES

Two Rivers

Umbria, Italy

Two rivers come together,
somehow finding one another
in the enchanting fog at dawn.

One meanders in
from the east,
reflecting on the meaning
of her journey
through many turns
of happiness and loss.

The other rushes in
from the west,
bright and enthusiastic
from his quick trip
down mountain valleys
that tried to lend guidance.

The wisdom
in the deep currents
of the one,
the determination
in the swift currents
of the other,
their fates
become intertwined
into one great river
that only now
can find its way
south to the sea.

Landscapes

I have been wandering
for so long across plains
so vast that mere days
expand into decades,
striving to fill the void.

An ocean of wheat and grass
swells across the expanse,
is drawn into waves
by wind and moonlight.

Errant ravines wander across
red deserts of stone and sand,
channels of invisible rivers
searching for the sound of water.

A blue horizon of mountains,
touched by the whiteness of snow,
reaches up into the clouds
cloaked in mystery.

My longing expands to the horizon
creating yet another landscape.
My pleas are amplified
by the grace of Earth
and echo as songs of desire.

Conversation With My Soul

Ghost Ranch, New Mexico

I met the hidden partner in my soul
as I walked along a lonely path
on the edge of a great wilderness.

There was a gentle, open light
all around her, flowing softly
from her kind, gracious eyes.

Bypassing all pleasantries, I said
"There is a great light around you,
I want to touch and embrace it."

We spoke for an instant, a day.
My fears and regrets became intimacy,
my darkness had eyes and I whispered

"You know the poetry of life,
walking through time with an open heart;
I see the divine I first glimpsed as a child.

You breathe a quiet, powerful spirit,
at times for me a shadow in the mists
over this wide, hard wilderness."

My soul was very modest and,
unaccustomed to lavish praise, said
"Enough, tell me of the gifts entrusted to you."

By then we had journeyed to the shores
of a mysterious lake whose name was
bittersweet waters of divine wisdom.

She bent gracefully toward me and said
"You cannot take in all the ocean at once,
you cannot get your arms around light.

You must let the light come in slowly
around the shadows of the mountains
and into the crevices of your being.

As with these cliffs, you must feel water seep
through fissures eons long, unseen inside rock,
that in its hardness has defeated centuries.

These cliffs cannot resist quiet drops
trickling down at the speed of dreams
to the depths of your secret well."

Sometimes We Wander Away

Sometimes we wander away from ourselves.
Sometimes the path drifts off ever so slightly
and we follow it without a hint of doubt,
at first just lost in thought or conversation.

Then, confident in our modestly errant steps,
we refuse to trace our way back to familiar terrain.
Instead of moving to the sanctuary of high ground
we saunter downhill towards a great thicket of doubt,
disguised by distance as a green valley of promise.
So, for years and years, we take our direction
from semblances, misconceptions, fantasies, mirages.

Then, we begin to wander back home,
guided at first by traces of the wind
in the sands of the desert that was our refuge,
then enticed by the scent of the distant shore,
drawn to the course suggested by ocean swells.
The far coast that beckons in our new dreams
is sometimes hidden by fog and misgivings.
Dark valleys drape off the brightening peaks beyond
like roads searching for direction, gathering aspiration.

Then, we receive a gift, a kind of grace,
a kind of light and can see a new landscape
that our wise hearts have always remembered.
So we move slowly on, inspired by wind traces,
drawn by the scent of water and mountain light
towards our heaven inside which we will gently carry,
grateful for new passion, for tears that foretell joy.

Plains of Castilla

Segovia, Spain

Plains of Castilla
graced by sheer,
dusty green ravines.
A reluctant rain
wanders into town,
sweetening the scent
of honeysuckle that flows
over palace walls,
etched by history.

Sounds of sensuous water
from the river deep below
are borne by waves of air
up graceful cliffs,
polished by centuries of wind.

Swallows rest for an instant
in the air—
an abundant maze
of dark stars
in the daylight sky—
then rise by delicate wings
on dense echoes of church bells
magnified by the canyons below,
all pointed at my heart.

Reflections

Ghost Ranch, New Mexico

Drawn in by the outstretched arms
of a gnarled tree at the edge of a meadow
two wanderers are joined by kind chance.
As they rest, they share their truths.
One says: "I see reflections
of God in your gracious eyes."
The other replies: "What you
see are faces of the Divine
on your own still waters."

For days and months of a new life
they continue their conversation,
as the eager seeds in the meadow
make their introductions with the ground.
All reflect upon the whereabouts
of clouds and rain, of happiness
and fulfillment, until their long discourse
bears the sweet fruit that was inside each.

Humble Water

Tiny springs toil all night,
eking precious water
through miserly cracks
inside hills of buried stone.

Rivulets join hands
in the reticent light of dawn
and wander through the forest,
searching for kindred water.

The stream finds its way
to the village you call home,
gathering reflections of love,
innocent as the meandering water.

Later, following a larger plan,
canyons the river has cut
focus the assembled memories
into wild dreams.

After creating canyons and dreams,
this great river begins to meander,
looking for a place to rest
after centuries of effort.

Eventually this humble water
brings a kiss of sweetness to the sea
then rises in gentle mists
and returns to the springs of her birth,
inspired by the wisdom of her journey.

Into the Labyrinth

Chartres, France

The labyrinth is a great circle,
radiating a soft invitation
from its narrow entrance
to pilgrims of life, wandering
in search of themselves.

Leave your puzzled mind outside,
wandering aimlessly
in a maze of its own
as it looks for finite answers
to the wrong questions.

Inside the sacred vessel,
in the suggestive light, a path
leads quickly towards the center
then out, by turns, to the periphery,
offering several glimpses inside.

Passersby glance in, looking
for that which eyes cannot see.
There is only one way in.
At the core truth waits,
as silent and patient as the stars.

Pilgrims walk north, south, east, west,
all moving towards the sacred middle,
approaching, meeting, pondering
visions from various passages:
birth, youth, maturity, death.

The journey inside is long
with many unexpected turns
for the student and teacher inside,
with as many questions as answers,
all illuminated by the window to truth.

Around the last bend to the center,
each pilgrim is greeted not by crowds
but by his own courageous soul,
waiting by the shores of silence,
gathering shadow, contradiction, light.

We are following the way of light,
tracing a path through swirling sands
along an ancient course almost forgotten.
Outside a desert; inside cleansing waters.
It is time to drink from a different cup.

The Laying of Hands

Ship set to leave, an emigre stands on the dock
with his mother, never to see each other again:
a promise to keep hearts close across oceans, yearning.

Two wanderers meet by chance at a crossing of paths,
their many distinct aspirations coming together,
uncovered in talking, their fates joined by yearning.

Secrets are kept in many places: in a diary,
in a will, in a short love letter never sent,
in a friend's trust before a long journey, yearning.

During a long conversation he touches her face.
His hands, the same color as the life in her smile,
remind her of the first time he touched her, yearning.

Pictures in an old family scrapbook, memories
reaching back to the many gifts brought by joy and loss:
with the turn of each page, a smile, a sigh, yearning.

In our meeting again, which could have been in a dream,
we gently laid our hands over each other's hearts
which quickened with desire, then calmed with trust, yearning.

Rising Out of the Canyon

A day, a month, a year slowly passes,
of being with you, of being without you.

Out from the ledge of a great canyon
overlooking infinities of light and shadow,
there is a path winding down to the interior.

A pilgrimage marked by turns of color,
of insight, of mood; new views of the expanse,
of memories taking similar journeys inside.

Down at the dark bottom, a brief respite
by the water; gratitude flows like the river,
makes heavy feet light, spirits alight.

Dreams rise up through branches of the night,
rise up out of the canyon, floating to the ridge.

Thank you for taking in the scent of flowers,
in Spring, the delicate scent of promise.

Thank you for conversations, journeys
along winding paths of loss, darkness and hope,
each of us holding onto the same torch light.

Thank you for a sojourn along Autumn roads,
through the plains and mountain valleys
where our youth once lived, where dreams began.

Thank you for your bright, spirited light,
a ray of sun at solstice beaming into the recesses
of a dark, lonely cave that had become my home.

Thank you for being together in the full moonlight,
for pondering the edge between light and darkness.

Slowly Parting

When the earth was very young and enthusiastic,
a slight rift or two identified continents.
By inches and eons, there began a drifting away.

A heavy thunderstorm fills the horizon at night.
Its lightning contests the grandeur of the mountains.
At dawn, it gathers clouds down the valley, drifting away.

A child experiments with youth, forms different
pieces of wood, string and rags into a sailboat.
Set on an eddy, it slips downstream, drifting away.

Thrown out on the ocean by a fierce storm at midnight
a chunk of wood, its gnarls turning upon itself,
turns its back to the shore, begins drifting away.

A solitary raven returns to the high ridge
where other ravens used to gather, senses some
freedom in the wind, flies up, begins drifting away.

On a still lake in summer, lovers slowly part
by a silent push of their row boats from one another.
No oar dips to stop the motion drifting away.

How Do I Say Good Bye?

September 11, 2001

How do I say good bye
to you whom I have known
for a time so sweet?
Budded flowers at dawn opened
at the mere thought of you,
sending ecstasy into hives of bees.

Before you came to me
I saw only the gray in clouds
on the lonely expanse of days,
and on restrained nights,
only the solitude in moonlight.

Then, you brought me grace
as the dawn drapes light over mountains,
as the horizon brings depth to the day,
as the stars bring wonder to the night.

But in an instant you are gone;
a part of my soul is cut away.
With what unworthy words
can I send you my blessings?
With what unfinished song
can I sing my gratitude?

I remember our last embrace.
Now I embrace loneliness
and my memories of you.

Your arms have become sorrow and despair
which embrace me with an intimacy

I have not known and do not beckon.
My tears will flow each day
sending sweetness and salt
to the solitary sea.

Each day I will ask how I can live
without the sweet melody of your voice
or the kind light flowing from your eyes.

As the mournful dusk approaches I will ask
how I can face the deep blackness of the night
without the hope of ever seeing you again.

Irises

Irises, in deep velvety purple,
used to remind me of passion;
intense sensuality
awakening in Spring,
opening up to the world,
pulling ardor in;
O'Keeffe's paintings
bursting out from the canvas.

Now irises remind me
of mourning and undoing;
the color you wore on the last day;
hard purple draped over caskets,
over love buried in the ground
left to try and claw its way
towards light and air,
so it can live again.

The mountain's purple cast
no longer draws me up the path.
Head bowed,
I turn away, remembering
the ending color,
purple,
the color of all the days now
as I lie down before them.

Living in Two Worlds

New Year's Eve
Colorado-New Mexico border

A drop falls from a reluctant cloud
onto the spine of the Rockies
that at once divide the continent
into directions, east from west
and cross the border, north to south.
The drop does not know where to go,
which direction is the most true,
so as it splashes, it divides itself up
into the directions of its calling.

A second falls from the universe,
drops in at the confluence of centuries,
splits itself into two, partaking of each,
still adding its small contribution to time.

Water flows gently across many borders,
of principalities and provinces, of states and countries,
not knowing it crosses any line, or is the line:
each pure drop tastes salt as it enters the sea.

Air traces the water's flow across imaginary lines,
and sniffs a new sweetness with each change of scenery.

Water, time and air; each in their own direction
effortlessly meandering between different worlds,
each in their universe without borders.

In a Spring in a Storm

*Iva Bell Hot Springs,
Sierra Nevada, California*

Hot water comes up through fissures,
eager for a visit with the river.
The spring trickles into a steaming pool
that relaxes by the clear, cold river.
Warm, moist air rises,
mingling with the low clouds.

A storm has followed me to this remote spring.
The falling snow gathers itself and pushes me in
almost before my clothes seem to fall away.
Above the pool the flakes melt into the sultry air
in anticipation of becoming healing water.
Inside, there is barely comfortable room for two:
the earth and I sit beside each other in a storm.

My spreading arms touch up against the sides
of this tiny universe, this womb
which holds me, nurtures me, helps me
remember the simplicity of my birth.
I curl up as the snow falls more intently
and dip underwater, wishing for an umbilical cord
so I might take in the wonders of this womb world
for hours at a time, instead of only a minute.

My tired bones, muscles and spirit
are all reminded of their true natures;
all welcome their first pure memories.
As my grateful body uncurls out of the water,
I am born again into a different kind of religion,
one of becoming intimate with the earth,
of touching her and being touched,
her passionate caress sustaining me
through each new gathering storm.

I Find Myself Looking for You

Rocky Mountains,
Southern Colorado

I find myself looking for you along roads,
in places that have been graced by your light,
along paths of our lives, hoping they will cross,
at the low river bank, waiting for your waves.

You remain inside those open rooms of desire,
one with new windows, another with fresh paint,
the large one dark, pungent, mysterious:
house of longing with a maze of hallways.

I am a wanderer, walking day and night,
sometimes held up by cold and lonely winds,
always searching for the call that will well up

inside my breast, burst forth, its faint echo
guiding me to the place where love has been
waiting, hoping that time would soon uncover.

Flight 1010

Over Minnesota

My Father has just died.
As I fly home,
clouds below take on the shapes
of dreams and myth;
fierce dragons defy angels,
whose swords are raised in righteousness.
Good and evil encircle one another
in a billowy confrontation in the sky.

Light and shadow, whiteness and darkness
reach all the way to the immense horizon
until there is tranquility, calm reflection,
the grace of pure light reaching to the divine.
All of this was inside you,
is inside me,
is inside sadness,
is inside longing.

First Train to Chicago

I take the South Shore at dawn from South Bend on my first trip to Chicago. The corn fields look a little like home except the surrounding land is dressed in restful green, not the hard-working browns of the Southwest. Soon corn stalks grow into smokestacks and barns into tenement houses. The land grows sad. Graffiti, smog and ash cover everything, like a black flag draped over a coffin. Where, Chicago, is your vital center? Is the core so intense, so white hot, that the ashes of those consumed by you are spread onto your outskirts? I am looking for life, not traces of death, so I'm not getting off this train just yet.

The pace quickens. Compressed tenements and warehouses sling past as we move from periphery to downtown station. On the street, a man comes up to me, confused, asking for directions. I can only tell him: "Sorry, I don't know my way around either. Where you from?" He answers: "Just got out of the VA hospital at Marion." Never having seen him before, he is familiar. Reminds me of my dad who did time in the VA psych wards at Albuquerque and Fort Lyons after his mind came apart many times over in the Big War. This wanderer is surprised when I give him my spare cash. He walks off, at least now with a smile. I wander off in the opposite direction, towards the Loop. Trains pass overhead. Most trains I have seen have been on the ground so I hop on the next "L" for an elevated view of the City. Then I am drawn to the Lake. It is immense, this Lake Michigan, compared to merely big but more contained man-made lakes at Cochiti, Eagle Nest and Navajo back home. I can't see across to the opposite shore here. God-made lakes have more power.

By now the sun and humidity are high. Not even the slightest breeze brings coolness off the Lake. Where, oh where, is the Wind in this City? Looking for refuge, I take the L over to the Art Institute and meander through, like a river trying to find its way. Then I see Picasso's blue painting of the Old Guitarist. He is hunched over by life and misfortune, playing a soulful melody to the memory of a beautiful woman, her gaze forever etched in his mind. For hours that take up the rest of the day, I keep coming back to hear his beckoning song. On the last train back, I imagine her face and remember the land I left behind, back home, waiting for me.

Vine by the Seashore

It seems you left so quickly
that I could only mumble a few words
outside the rhythms of my heart.
It seems you will never hear
those ecstatic songs deep inside me
that search patiently for a voice.
It seems that I am left with
memories and dreams of life
in another place, at another time
unfolding into another form,
like ocean swells floating into waves
approaching a seashore long ago.

I say good bye to the places
where you once lived and dreamt:
to the mountains, cliffs and hills
that gently guided you on your way;
to the streams that later felt
all of your wistful meanderings;
to the beaches where you walked
along the boundary of earth and water;
to the landscapes in mist and fog
that mirrored your hazy contradictions;
to the valleys that gave you shadow and
to the dawn peaks that graced you with light.

There is happiness and there is loss,
intertwined like branches of a great vine
reaching up, supported only by hope
and by gnarled roots deeply set
in the earth of our beings
which were once joyful together.

I am anointed by waves of gratitude and peace.
I am the seashore welcoming the tide's advance,
understanding that the waves will be pulled away,
only to return with new, more adventurous sea foam.

Fishing for Truth

*Rio San Antonio,
New Mexico*

After my long walk in
on a path guided by
the gentle dawn
and the dreams
of the meandering valley,
I am ready to begin
my day on the river.

My rod sheds its casing
and asks for a line,
like an eager child
trying to step out of boredom
and into summer.

My guide for today is memory.
I'll try the patterns
and stretches of the river
that worked last year
at this time, on this water.

On top, a flighty little caddis
with a greenish brown body
and plenty of gray wing
to keep it floating
in swirling currents
of mystery and inspiraton.

For a dropper off the caddis
an even smaller peacock prince
from the green heaven of nymphs

where it was blessed
with a chameleon countenance
so it becomes with each second
what the fish want it to be.

So, to all you fish
holding in the secret currents,
I can wait for your attention
as hours wait for days,
as days wait for years.

My patience is greater
than the rocks along the bank
that endlessly guide the river.

I will dangle new meanings,
new drifts in every riffle,
new thoughts in every pool,
patiently floating ideas down river

while angling for insight
streaking up from the depths.
Eventually the fish,
sensing something real,
come up from their schools
for tiny bites of truth.
After a brief interlude,
I release them back to the depths
so we can all go on, searching.

Touching Joy

We were rivers, youthful, abundant, clear.
We flowed headlong through canyon destinies,
then meandered down valleys, wondering.
Our fragrant waters had not yet touched.

Now we have joined, the scenery has changed.
We flow slowly into each other at dawn.
A new face of the sun gazes towards us,
casts so much happiness, our waters glisten.

When I embrace you, I am touching joy,
am drawn by the generous light in your eyes,
your open heart, the dense pull of desire.

In your arms, mysteries reveal their secrets:
the yearning of two rivers coming together,
of stars exchanging their light across the night.

Ode to Apricots

Santa Fe

Early blossoms
of Spring,
early promise,
of pungent white,
braving frost.
Like frost,
draping a light veil
across valleys,
over villages,
full, bountiful,
gathering life with
the mere suggestion
of fruit, of apricots
in the making.

Sun and earth
add hints:
tartness
bursting out
in the middle
of future conversations;
passion, defiance,
exuberance and sweetness,
all hard to contain
in so small a vase.

Source of all yellow,
for coreopsis in later Spring,
for sunflowers in Summer,
all gathered by bees
for a feast in August.

Tiny mirrors of the sun,
color of the mountains
in Autumn,
seeds of amber light
dotted on every tree,
lending new hues
to country roads
lining the orchards.

Then, preserves.
In their making,
fruit on fruit mixed
with fire and water,
a little pectin,
and some wild aspirations
thrown in
for good measure.

Glowing enthusiasm
poured into jars.
Kitchens brighten,
even dark pantries
light up.
At breakfast,
a spoonful
of Spring,
a helping
of Summer.
Distilled wonder,
purity of gold,
intensity unbound,
eager to spread out
across December,
through Winter,
until it touches
Spring again.

Lighthouse of God

Mont St. Michel, France

Out on the horizon of fields,
beyond the waves of wheat,
the steeples of light rise up
through the mists of dawn.
The abbey atop the distant cliffs
is at the boundary of land and sea,
earth and heaven, memory and promise.

Wayfarers on their long journeys
can now put down their earthly maps,
can look past their years of wandering,
can turn away from their doubts
and begin to orient themselves
in the direction of repose
on the last day's walk towards truth.

Near the end of the sojourn
there is a slow spiraling climb
along a labyrinth of narrow streets,
through an array of lookouts,
each standing witness
to the legendary tide coming in
at the pace of a galloping horse.

The tide retreats almost as quickly,
leaving traces of itself
glimmering in the afternoon sand.
The abbey is now an island
surrounded not by water,
but by a million facets of light
in the sand, illuminating its old walls.

Up above, the path bends around
a final turn and, after a long struggle,
in an instant points to the top
of the lighthouse of God.

View from Joy

Montserrat
Cataluñia, Spain

The swirling mists,
the highest clouds,
carry devout water
kissed by bitter salt
in the deep darkness
of the stormy sea.

Weary pilgrims
silently cross
wandering canyons
and walk up to the church
at the top of the cliff
only to find
the height of their joy
measured by
the depth of their longing.

LOOKING HOME

Floating

When I was twelve, you taught me
the art of the jump shot out there
in the dirt driveway, old rusty rim
without a net evaluating my efforts,
"clank, clank, clank," while yours
sailed through the center of the rim,
"swish, swish, swish," through the net
of the air. I remembered your years
as a star player on your teams,
as the star player of my family.
Out there in the driveway
you talked about doing things
the right way, about feeling it.

"It's like this: bend your knees,
way down, ball at your waist,
jump up, in one motion bringing
the ball quickly above your head,
let the ball draw you up into the air,
up above the defenders as you focus
on the back of the rim, wrist cocked,
finger tips only on the ball seams,
extend your arm in an instant, high,
snap your wrist like you're waving
goodbye one last time because
you're sending that ball home,
where it wants to be."

And I saw you rising up, floating,
smiling, releasing the ball,
floating, towards its goal.
Then you turned, looked far away,

walked ever so quickly out of my day,
ever so slowly into my reflections
of that last day; into my dreams.

Every now and then in my life,
I remembered it just right, in your image.
There I'd be, in mid-game,
in mid-air, releasing the ball,
floating above the defenders
feeling the shot was good
as soon as it left my hand,
knowing I was sending it home
with that last, strong wave.

There I'd be in the middle of the night,
thinking about that Christmas
a couple of years after you left
where your spirit drew you home
but you stopped, disoriented,
exhausted from a long journey
through mountains and across plains,
then laid down under a lonesome piñon,
your body becoming as frozen as
the ground upon which you lay.

You float between memory and dreams,
a bright cloud moving across the sky,
lending depth to the landscape.
I see you rising above the crowd, focused,
intense, seeing what others could not see;
releasing a busy life in the city,
guiding yourself to a serene monastery,
isolated in a mountain valley,
vowing to be closer to God, who is inside;

knowing the importance of good bye,
that each one could be the last,
and the lasting memory we each carry;
a bright star floating slowly across the night.

Letter to My Son

You struggled to come into this world,
holding back as if to prepare me
for immense joy.
The doctor finally cut things short
by cutting you out from the womb
to save your life.
If you had died that day,
a part of me, or all of me,
would have followed you
as your companion.

Instead, your birth gave me
new and abundant life.
When the nurse brought you
through the operating room door
and into my arms, you were
the color of sandstone in early light.
I tenderly embraced you
and as I kissed you for the first time
you breathed delicate air
across my face
and deep into my heart.

When you looked at me
for the first time, I saw
the gray eyes of my father
and a life filled with grace.

Finding My Father

I remember long river days
where I wandered and gazed
along a meandering path,
hoping that I could find you.

You were taken from me many times,
first by incessant hallucinations of war
that you re-lived during many brutal days,
then by obscure nights studying history
that only shed more darkness on the past.

You were taken from me many times,
by day and by night, then by a straight jacket,
new white suit brought by hospital orderlies,
whiteness which could not impose order
on the gathering darkness of mental illness.

Then you were taken by the kind reaper of death
who visited after you had already died a thousand deaths,
who closed your eyes to the endless brutality of war,
and finally returned a youthful smile to your face
as you looked for the first time into peaceful light.

Where are you? Can I find you in my memories
which echo in place of your heartbeats?
There, you are sweeter than the apples
you picked for me in your father's orchard.

Can I find you in my dreams
which reveal your true image?
There, you are compassionate and bright,
unshackled from the irons of illness.

There, your deep sorrows and joys
are rendered by mysterious blessings
into illuminating letters buried with you,
waiting for me to come digging.

I remember long rivers of grace
where I walked inside dreams and memories,
truth moving in my blood that is yours,
woven in my bones that are yours.

Helping Ida

My mother was born in the country
of a family as humble as the ditch
that brought simple water
by the houses and into the fields;
of parents as enchanting as the moon
that graced the night sky each month
and brought soft light into every home.

Her favorite question of the day
to her mother, who treated her as a sister,
asked what Ida could do to help:
with hearth fires that took frost off windows
and put crust on loaves of kneaded bread;
or with the hoe that put furrows in the fields
and guided ditches through the orchards.

In return, her world came to her for help,
cousins and nieces, friends and nephews,
brothers and uncles, strangers and sisters,
father, mother, husband, daughter and son.
She helped some to read, write or respect,
some to be good parents to their children,
some to be good children to their parents.

She brought joy to Christmas, hope to Spring
when each might otherwise not have come.
As sister, she was also mother to her siblings.
She comforted fearful and weary travelers.
There were all of her family and friends
who learned to walk with illness or death,
for a month, a year or a lifetime.

My mother lived through many deaths,
of family, of friendships, of trust;
of her marriage, of independence, of faith.
She was a teacher of many lonesome souls,
her lessons learned by listening to solitude.
In the end the multitudes came for a year,
all holding her hand, returning favors, helping Ida.

Ode to My Quilt

The source of all color,
universe of stories
patched together
by gravity of memory,
woven into life tones.
Brilliant chaos flowing
from every edge.
A blanket worthy
of caressing light.
My quilt,
well of color
fed by a spring
trickling upwards
as if through
buried plumes
of volcanic stone
into the warm pool
of my bed.

My comforter,
bringing light
into darkness:
light treasure
in the trunks
of voyagers
sailing seas
of destiny;
a candle in the
cold loneliness
of a dreary castle;
protector of pioneers
huddled in wagons

against waves
of drifting snow.

Intimate friend
who has touched me,
purifying my mistakes,
rendering dreams vibrant;
companion who has held me
through fearful nights,
who has embraced me
with the promise of morning.

Mosaic of memories:
curtains
from my mother's kitchen;
pieces
from my grandfather's suits;

pants
from my father's travels;
threads
from my grandmother's dreams.
Collection
of remnants,
shards of colorful pottery
from an ancient civilization,
wise in its simplicity.

I covered myself
with this patchwork,
draped myself
with casts of life,
with cloth made soft
by love,

my quilt,
transformed
by the hands of angels
into a rainbow
of grace.

Tending the Dead

Many tombstones, many ashes,
all cold and gray in the ground.
Small part of my family,
large part of my heart;
partly in this world,
mostly in another.

My uncle, ill-fitting uniform
of a military grave,
tombstone askew, others straight.
True grave under a lonesome pine
alongside a wandering, forlorn road.
While hitching a ride home for Christmas
he sleepily laid down one stark night
for a rest that became eternal.
Yellow narcissus for Friendship.
Hearty blooms in the frigid snow,
obsessed with their yellowness,
immune from freezing or death.

My father, same cemetery, confused
amidst uneasy markers of death.
Stone covering a vibrant mind
split in two at twenty;
grave injustice of a just war.
Mental illness, sickness of the soul,
brought him many deaths,
more than there are gravestones here.
Red roses for Passion.
Petals to cover his heart;
love which he could not embrace,
colorful shield against grays of fear.

My mother, under a heavy cross,
slowly carried with quiet courage
through crowds of loss.
Fair woman of the cross,
nun turned caretaker
of many yearning families,
another kind of mother superior;
protector; strict enforcer of truth.
Lilacs for Hope.
Bright promise of Spring
covering many faces of death,
vibrant through layers of doubt.

My grandfather, well-suited to his place
near the hills we used to walk;
peacefully resting in a bed made for two,
covers lying open, beckoning his wife.
Keeper of books, miner of memories,
accompanied by a grateful family,
by friends meandering along the river
and the soulful tunes of his harmonica.
Wild flowers for Joy.
For the wandering poet of life
who carried me in his arms
across hidden paths of his heart.

Many tombstones, a few souls,
now bright in the ground.

You Are the Gift

The seasons bring their abundant gifts:
birth, rain, transformation, snowy repose.

Waves and starlight come in night and day
suggesting their gifts of infinite grace.

Birthdays, anniversaries and holidays
bring their gifts of promise and renewal.

On this day when your light brings me new hope
time and memory let me know that you are the gift.

That Last Evening

That last evening
amidst the city lights,
amidst the reflections
the flowers and the laughter,
I wanted to stretch out time:
seconds into conversations,
minutes into ruminations,
dusk into a long, joyful night.

I moved, embrace by embrace,
across the evening landscape
wanting to know your life's story,
hoping that in its telling,
memories would reach out
from the depths of your past
and sketch the outline of your dreams.

I meandered through time
like a river finding its way
through many turns,
at once washing up
against opposite banks—
doubt and longing,
fear and hope—
each suggesting a new direction
but with different aspirations
of unbounded life out at sea.

To My Child Never Born

You were the first trickle
of a spring that will never flow
up from calm depths
held by the Creator of water.
The name of my grandmother
who first held me
and sweet rain
would have been your name.

You are the first light
of a galaxy so infinitely remote
its sight will never reach earth.
Graceful illumination would have
swirled vividly inside you,
would have taught darkness to sing,
would have turned itself into pure light
each time you opened your eyes.

You are the grand symphony
played intently in the mind
of the composer who is deaf,
struck down at the last note.
You are the soulful poet
who will never search for truth
buried beneath miscarriage
or carried in mists above the seas.

You are inside me, seeing with my eyes,
vibrant with each beat of my heart,
taking your first hesitant steps,
walking quietly alongside me
towards friendship, marriage, truth.

You are a child of life embracing itself,
powerful, brilliant, enlightened.
All of my days thinking of you
are my grandchildren, born anew
born of you, bringing me gifts.

Gratitude

Winter sent me
my parents' gray deaths
and bright memories
of their lives.

Spring brings me
the promise of dreams
as white-blossomed trees
dream of cherries.

I honor Summer
for days as long as rivers
and for journeys of my heart
into the past.

I am grateful to Autumn
for mountains of amber light,
for my birthday,
and for you.

You Are Inside Me

You are inside me today, this hour.
Our hearts beat an enchanting rhythm:
drums on the shore of my chest
pounding in time with the waves.

You are the pulse of my earth body,
waves of rain surging into a river
arousing new desires: for clear lakes,
a long run to the coast, your gaze.

Your eyes are oceans unfurling their pensive
infinities against my shores, moving
through my body, disregarding boundaries:

desire and embrace, earth and water,
starlight and dawn, dream and daylight,
my memories of you and tomorrow.

Gazing Toward the Horizon of Hope

At the ledge the landscape opens up to a view
where ancestors once struggled, of heart memories,
and silence falls after a sigh, that's how you know.

When she imagines what he does in the morning
though his sun is on the other side of the world
and only deep stars are over her, that's how you know.

Where the people search for a bridge from fear to hope,
when the leader's urgent appeals are tinged with God,
but inside his altar is godless, that's how you know.

When his stirring anger deepens into hatred,
where his refusal to forgive becomes a dagger
that he turns towards his own heart, that's how you know.

In an exchange between a judge and a lawyer
or a lawyer and witness at trial, there is a glance
up to truth or down to lies, that's how you know.

When at the mere thought of her, on hearing her name
he smiles, gazes toward the dim horizon of hope
and the landscape quickly brightens, that's how you know.

My Son Is Coming Home

Winter Solstice

All I need is for my son to come home.
My quiet longing for him rises again,
magnifies the months he has been gone
into years, stretches time into decades.

His light is coming towards me this hour,
this darkest day of the year, this longest night,
when the promise of his light is just enough,
when, for an instant, it replaces the dawn.

I bend the orbit of earth, of hope circling
the sun, so that time pulls at a new pace,
quickened by the deep gravity of love,

so that he can be carried even faster
across continents, seas and memories,
into the landscape of my waiting heart.

Ode to My Shovel

On my birthday,
in the mountains,
my grandmother gave me
my grandfather's shovel.
A shovel bearing treasures
that she uncovered
and honed
in her wisdom and love.

I left my grandfather
for manhood
in his grave
cut by this shovel
and filled again,
by turns,
with mounds
of bittersweet earth.
This shovel,
which toiled with him
in his lifetime,
toiled again,
as it spaded dirt
upon his burial ground.
On my birthday,
on his death day,
his shovel, my shovel,
that of every man,
came alive before us.

Its old wooden handle,
was rough in places,
as the calloused hands
that grasped it

during days of long labor.
Its hardened steel scoop
tempered in impersonal furnaces,
infinitely more tempered by life
in all of the intimate places.

In fields of dawn,
digging for new crops.
In trenches troweling stone
for foundations of new houses.
In orchards planting trees,
for fruits of passion
and a life rich in spirit.
In all of the intimate places.

In deep mines of darkness,
digging for the blackness of coal.
In ditches begging hills for water.
In mountains of light,
leveling pathways and roads,
all searching for a home.
In all of the intimate places.

In countless graves,
dredging sorrow and remembrance
for children buried early,
for brothers and sisters
taken from the arms of their lovers,
for mothers and fathers
resting from their perilous journeys.

My shovel is a fine instrument
tuned to the rhythms of life,
and to thunderous echoes of earth
heaped onto pine coffins.

We are all standing
on the grave of our ancestors,
reaching down
to ground made of bones.
As we raise the dry soil
that sifts finely
through our cradling fingers,
we offer an incense of dust
and delve gently into the tomb
that slowly bears our souls.

NEW PASSAGES

We Saw the Moon Rise

After a long day's journey
to the place you call home,
to the place I call home,
we took in the expanse at dusk
by a high mountain meadow
ringed by blue spruce and piñon,
waiting to meet the full moon.

The expanse of the meadow,
of the day, suggested life,
suggested memories of other days,
of the plains, meadows,
mountains and other places
where our ancestors walked,
rested and laid down in death.

In their telling, our stories
of struggles and dreams,
of life and loss, became blessings
and thanksgiving, brought
new light over the dimming
landscape, expanded dusk
and the fading outline of the meadow.

Expanded them just enough
to make room for the day and night,
just enough to make room
for the past and the future
to join in that instant
where moonlight touches
the soft light of evening.

We saw the full moon rise
up through the trees, up through
the clouds that opened just enough
to pass the moonlight through
to our open, waiting hearts,
just enough to let in the fullness
of the gathering night.

Passages

I have crossed oceans
and moored in foggy ports,
trying to find a home for my heart.

My struggles are skeletons
piled into a heap as high
as my heart memories are deep.

I have walked across deserts,
against winds crying out
for a calm place to stay.

It took time to take in
the buoyancy of light
after wandering through darkness.

I have lived by the pensive sea,
on plains reclining out to the horizon
and in mountains touching the clouds.

Occasionally, time just trickled by.
At other times, years passed
and I awakened as if from a dream.

Now I am poised for passage
to even more intimate places
where I feel grace pulsing in my blood,
where I see the faces of God everywhere,
and remember the blessings of my journey
as I am born into these new worlds.

Gather All of Yourself

You have crossed great waters
searching for frontiers up ahead,
longing for truth in the mists.

Once on land, you walked for years
across landscapes of hope and ruin,
dossals woven by light and darkness.

Now, the colors of your dreams
have banded together into a rainbow,
into a diploma of light waiting for you.

So pause and gather all of yourself
before kissing the sweet stone of faith
at the shrine on top of the hill.

You are on the holy ground of happiness:
soft, grateful, whispering greetings
in quiet celebration of your arrival.

Thanksgiving

After war took my father
the peace in your eyes
descended into my heart,
turning resentment to forgiveness.

You are the healing river
wending its patient way
through the vastness of time,
determined to sweeten the bitter sea.

You are the kindness
that embraces strangers
and brings a smile
to their now hopeful faces.

You are the sweetness
of fruit on Autumn days
that I imagine as I walk
through Spring orchards in bloom.

I Want to Dance

After the long journey
filled with quiet reflection
and the search for truth inside
that gives way to love,
the wanderer turns
a hopeful gaze outside,
upwards through darkness,
and sees two heavenly bodies
slowly drawn together
by the gravity of fate,
the kind pull of happiness.

One approaches the other
like a great comet
that slowly brightens
in its celestial orbit
and becomes brilliant
in anticipation
of its ecstatic rendevous
with the sun,
with the face of light,
which it has sought
for centuries.

My heart knows
what it knows.
May I have this dance
with you?

What Is This Longing?

What is this longing that slowly draws
sweetness from a field without flowers,
that draws light around shadow,
that draws me to you, then
out into the rain looking for a rainbow,
out through the night as if to the stars?

Explorers set out, following the sun
eventually bringing home a rough new map.
Continents are not quite the same:
limitless oceans have found new shores;
deserts, mountains and rivers add grace
to the landscapes. Dreams are more vivid.

Out on the pilgrimage, a few friends,
many souls, all moving in one direction.
Their path ascends to a different place
where there is no path, no footing,
no markings along the perilous way
but the edge between light and darkness.

Companions, not quite lovers yet,
sit beneath a tree, resting, wandering
through a day's journey into conversation.
Light and shadow cross their faces,
light wraps around shadow in their hearts,
the way an embrace covers hesitation, fear.

In my dream, I slowed the passage of light,
stretched it out across time and memory,
saw the brilliant traces of its rainbow colors.
I traced its passage as if through a prism,
through me and out along a long journey
to all of the places I hoped to find you.

Quiet Courage

Outside, there are no signs of great heroics.
Children are not plucked from fiery rooftops,
nor shocked travelers from raging waters,
nor dazed residents from the rubble of fallen homes.
Valiant soldiers do not save the honor of their countries.
There are no dazzling medals, no proud statues
to commemorate the slaying of the dragon.

Inside, there is a silent struggle with doubt and faith.
The solitary path comes up to steep cliffs of fear.
Beyond, a sea of loneliness swirls all around;
regret is in the depths, the horizon hazy.
On the far side of the inside world, light waits
with infinite patience to embrace you, sojourner,
voyager of emotion, bearer of simple truths,
who have come across the last abyss
on wings of quiet courage, finding your way at last.

How Long?

How long does it take
for sand to walk across the desert?

How long does it take
for fog to climb the highest mountain?

How long does it take
for water to sail around the world?

How long until
ice in the north sea goes south for the winter?

How long before
a volcano rouses in the early morning to see a fiery sunrise?

When does
the darkness of coal awaken to the clarity of a diamond?

How long before
a continent travels across the ocean to visit the place of its birth?

When do
waves stop asking the coastline if it can change its look again?

How long does it take
for small blocks of years to build up a mountain range?

How long until
a single crack works its way to bring a mountain down?

How long before
a rainbow sells its colors to flowers in the darkest jungle?

How long before
the wind from the far side of the world gestures that all is well?

How many rings does it take
for a tree to become betrothed to the earth?

How long until
you wander through all the secret pathways of my heart?

How long does it take
for your sweet light to come across the room and greet me?

I Will Be With You

I will be with you, sorrowfully,
when your father and mother
who held you so tenderly
are themselves first held
by the cold darkness of ground;
when, in your loneliness,
you walk the path of an orphan
and let your cries of heartache
go out over mourning fields.

I will be with you, joyfully,
when your mother and father
converse in the language of dreams
and you wistfully embrace them
in the heaven of memories;
when, in your happiness,
they gaze upon you
from the eyes of your children,
from yours in the truthful mirror.

Let Your Sweetness In

Inside you there is a flower
whose sweet dreams all day long
attract an excited following
of hummingbirds and bees.

Before offering these passersby
a taste of their aspirations,
let your sweetness
seep even deeper inside
until the one who kisses you
tastes the intensity of life
on your hopeful lips.

Fifty

Fifty is what I am today,
first seeing age in my life.

Fifty times around the sun,
trying to find my way.

Fifty years tracing out time,
being reborn, yet growing older.

Fifty times past winter solstice,
hard darkness taking me inside.

Fifty times past summer solstice,
abundant light showing me promise.

At my mother's tomb, I thank her for life,
and for teaching me how to hope for light.

At my father's grave, I thank him for life,
and for showing me how to touch darkness.

With my wife, we take in life
with song and poetry in our hearts.

My son's voice on a call from afar
carries his light back to me.

My sister and our memories
take me back through shared time.

In darkness I have given away time,
have held back some gifts.

Some days I have tried to hold light,
have felt grace inside time's passage.

In darkness I have loved
but haven't loved enough.

I am each year. I am a half century.
I am in darkness reaching for light.

Blessings

1.
A small seed patiently waits in the cone,
a rough and gnarled womb on the ground.
For years the seed knows only darkness,
but after being blessed by an immense fire,
it grows up into the clouds as a powerful tree.

2.
Last night I dreamt an angel
brought you the kind of happiness—
the deep happiness that becomes joy—
that is known by a mother and father
as they hold their new-born child.

3.
After traveling for many very different years,
after seeking the shelter of many lonesome roads,
the wandering minstrel eventually finds a home;
inside his heart are the rhythms, the sweet notes
he first hears as he rests in the shade of his solitude.

Stories of Our Lives

At a refuge near a mountain pass
two pilgrims come in from the cold,
their solitary spirits slowly join
as they begin their inquiries into
the gravity of companionship
after years alone out on the road.
The night conspires with a storm
to hold them together longer.
Their stories become intimate.
After clouds and darkness move on,
each pilgrim is drawn to a different
horizon and they move on, searching.

At a small crossroads near twilight
old acquaintances exchange glances,
hear new comfort in each other's voices
as they begin walking along the same road.
The evening transforms decades apart
into as many stories as there were years.
Over a few months, many hours
of long days and even longer nights
are taken up as they each reflect
the other's light, the other's darkness.
Each is a godsend, bringing the godsend
of hope to their remaining lifetime together.

At a small clearing near Autumn,
I stop for a while to be with my shadow,
my only companion, who follows as closely
as the specter of repose that slowly begins
to shroud the valley below in reds and yellows,
the hues drawing me deeper into life.

I gaze far past early snow on the peaks
toward Spring, wondering if its lonely winds
will scatter my memories of you across
the high desert near where you once lived,
hoping it's promise will accompany me
and my shadow on our journey back to you.

In the many stories of our lives,
in their telling, years are marked
by minutes, passages marked by images,
as our unwavering hearts beat on
loving what they love, whom they love,
outside the passage of time.

I Thought I Knew Love

I thought I knew love.
I was content taking in
the expanse of the horizon at dawn
and at dusk, releasing it back to the night.
My heartbeats were measured,
in tune with the songs of birds in the trees.

Then you came bearing gifts
of grace, passion and truth.
The pathways of my heart became intimate.
We walked through mists of old doubt
and there found a passage of new faith.
We became comfortable in the darkness
because there we also found light.

Now, the horizon is inadequate.
My heart is attuned to the infinite symphony
of waves at the seashore in the night.
I feel beauty in the darkest crevices
of the earth, below the ocean,
underneath still water in the depths.
My love is no longer measured,
except by the space taken up by stars.

Coming Home

There are different greetings coming home,
from my family, my friends, the mountains.
There is new light in the old neighborhood.

The shades of my mother's hair have turned
from light black to gray, even bright white,
as have the tones of my father's countenance.

Every now and then, an old friend drops in
unexpectedly, ready for a new conversation.
The geography of relationship is different.

Even the mountains have changed a little.
A new hue of lichen slowly spreads on cliffs.
The river meanders, is more contemplative.

One ridge has grown up with the trees,
another has dropped down by a rockslide,
their fortunes changing, like reputations.

One person has moved up to a new place,
another walks slowly, with a slight limp.
Others have worn down into the ground.

I have left the place of angular talking
where light was interrupted, hemmed in
by steel buildings rising over sidewalks.

I am coming home, drawn in by faith,
by a change of scenery, by my calling,
comfortable with a new change of clothes.

I am coming home where there is new light,
where conversations begin along familiar lines
but soon turn to a different path circling deeply

through old memories, new reflections,
through vast new interior landscapes,
over to that place where hope lives.

We Had More to Say

We each had more to say.
Somewhere along the way
our words gave way to silence.
Out of nowhere—or everywhere—
in a story, in a sentence.

An artist sketches the landscape,
the confluence of lines
hints at a presence
beyond the canvas,
an image as vague as mist,
a likeness without a name.

After snow falls
it melts and comes down
from its high mountain perch,
trying to sing a new song
that it has not yet composed.
A spring, a river, ocean waves.

After a great storm,
the clouds stumble
over one another
trying to rearrange themselves
into a semblance of snowy mountains
or a foggy coastline.

The intimate silence seemed to linger
but only stayed for an instant
filled with longing and hope.
The quiet elicited more
than our elusive words.

ABOUT THE AUTHOR

Raymond Z. Ortiz is a native of Santa Fe with deep roots in Northern New Mexico where his extended family and ancestors have lived for over four centuries. His was first inspired by poetry as a child listening to his grandfather recite poems in the shade of a willow after a long day of chores. Poetry has been an integral part of his life since then, initially as he continued listening and reading, then as a student of poetry and literature. He received his BA from the University of Notre Dame, then lived in Costa Rica while volunteering as a social worker. He continued his formal education at the University of California Berkeley (Boalt Hall) where he received his JD.

After clerking for a New Mexico Supreme Court Justice for two years, he practiced law for over twenty years, first as an associate, then as a partner in the same firm. In late 2005 he was appointed district court judge by the Governor. Long before this time, he found his voice as a poet. Even with a demanding law practice, the hour before dawn would often find him at a table in a dark part of the house, writing out poems in longhand by candlelight. He continues his poetic endeavors, although at shorter intervals before dawn. Over the years, his poetry and short stories have been published in regional journals and anthologies. This is his first book.